*Every day is a good day
if you pray -*

Alberta Woodring

NEW TESTAMENT STORIES

NEW TESTAMENT STORIES

RETOLD FOR CHILDREN

By
Lillie A. Faris

Author of
Standard Bible Story Readers
Old Testament Stories Retold for Children

Illustrated by
Arthur O. Scott

·NEW·YORK·
·THE·PLATT·&·MUNK·CO· INC·

Copyright MCMXL,
By
THE PLATT & MUNK CO., INC.
Made in U. S. A.

FOREWORD

ANY life is incomplete without a study of the life and teachings of Jesus. As this book of New Testament Stories comes to you, it brings many lovely stories of the life of your very best friend—Jesus. You will understand as you read these stories how dearly He loved boys and girls, and I am sure you will want to grow like Him—pure, good and unselfish.

There are stories, too, of some of Jesus' best helpers—fine, strong, courageous men, who were not afraid to do as they were told.

In writing these stories for you I have tried to picture your eager faces as you read the wonder-story, of a blind man who received his sight, or some crippled man whose ankles became strong and well, and I have fancied you saying, "Oh, how wonderful Jesus is and how I love Him!"

Then, too, there are the pictures you will love. They are so true to the story and they all carry a beautiful thought.

It is my deep abiding wish that, as these stories were selected and written in a vocabulary easily mastered by a child under twelve years, you may readily react to their influence and your life become fuller and richer.

LILLIE A. FARIS

CONTENTS

NEW TESTAMENT

	Page
THE ANGEL'S MESSAGE TO MARY	13
THE MANGER CRADLE	17
THE BABY JESUS IN THE TEMPLE	21
THE WISE MEN AND THE STAR IN THE EAST	24
THE FLIGHT INTO EGYPT	28
THE VISIT TO JERUSALEM	30
JOHN THE BAPTIST AND JESUS	32
JESUS AND THE NOBLEMAN'S SON	35
HEALING THE CRIPPLE AT BETHESDA	37
JESUS AND THE FISHERMEN	39
THE SERMON ON THE MOUNT AND THE BEATITUDES	40
WHAT JESUS TAUGHT ABOUT PRAYER	43
THE TWELVE APOSTLES	46
THE WIDOW'S SON	48
"PEACE BE STILL"	50
THE RULER'S DAUGHTER	52
FEEDING THE FIVE THOUSAND	55
JESUS WALKING ON THE WATER	58
JESUS MAKES A BLIND MAN SEE	60
THE TRANSFIGURATION	63
THE GOOD SHEPHERD	65
JESUS BLESSES LITTLE CHILDREN	68
THE RICH YOUNG RULER	71
ZACCHAEUS—A MAN WHO WAS SORRY	72
MARY AND MARTHA	74
JESUS BRINGS LAZARUS BACK TO LIFE	75
MARY'S GIFT FOR JESUS	77
THE TRIUMPHAL ENTRY	78
THE GOOD SAMARITAN	79
JUDAS BETRAYS JESUS	83
CHRIST BEFORE PILATE	87
THE CRUCIFIXION	90
JESUS LIVING AGAIN	92
THE WALK TO EMMAUS	95
DOUBTING THOMAS	97
A BEGGAR AT THE BEAUTIFUL GATE	99
PHILIP AND THE ETHIOPIAN	101
DORCAS, A FRIEND OF THE POOR	105
STEPHEN	107
ANANIAS AND SAPPHIRA	108
PAUL AND SILAS IN PRISON	110
PAUL IN EPHESUS	113
PAUL'S SHIPWRECK	115
A SLAVE WHO RAN AWAY	119
JOHN'S VISION ON THE ISLAND OF PATMOS	121

THE ANGEL'S MESSAGE TO MARY

IN a little town called Nazareth, in a country far away across the sea, lived a beautiful girl, named Mary. Mary's eyes were dark. Her hair was dark, too, and long and shining.

Mary used to sing as she went about her work. She loved to sing the songs that King David had written: "The Lord is my Shepherd," and "O give thanks unto Jehovah, for he is good."

Often in the evening Mary would go up the steps, on the outside of her house, to the little flat roof. There she would stand and look out, over the whole village of Nazareth.

Then she would look beyond the village, to the mountains in the distance.

She loved to lift her eyes to the blue sky and watch the stars come out.

Mary often talked to God in the quiet of the evening and asked Him to help her to be good and kind and true.

And the Father in heaven heard her prayer.

It must have been that He found no one so gentle, kind and pure as Mary, because He planned for her, the most wonderful thing that had ever happened to anyone.

The Father had promised, that some day He would send His Son to the earth, and when the time drew near for His coming, He said, "Mary shall be His mother."

One day God called His angel, Gabriel, and asked him to tell Mary.

The angel must have been very proud and happy, to carry such a joyful message.

Gabriel found Mary in her little home in Nazareth and he said to her, "God has blessed you greatly."

"You are to be the mother of God's Son and you shall call His name Jesus.

"He shall be great and he shall be called, the Son of the most high.

"He shall be the greatest king that ever lived, for he shall reign forever."

The angel's words made Mary very happy; she did not quite understand all that he said, but she knew that God had blessed her.

Mary could not keep the good news to herself, so she set off at once to see her cousin, Elisabeth, to tell her about the angel's visit.

THE ANGEL SAID TO HER, "GOD HAS BLESSED YOU GREATLY."

Here is the beautiful song that Mary sang to thank the Father in heaven:

"My soul doth magnify the Lord,
  And my spirit hath rejoiced in God my Saviour.
For he hath regarded the low estate of his handmaiden:
For, behold, from henceforth all generations shall call me blessed.
For he that is mighty hath done to me great things;
And holy is his name.
And his mercy is on them that fear him from generation to generation.
He hath shewed strength with his arm;
He hath scattered the proud in the imagination of their hearts.
He hath put down the mighty from their seats,
And exalted them of low degree.
He hath filled the hungry with good things;
And the rich he hath sent empty away.
He hath holpen his servant Israel,
In remembrance of his mercy;
As he spake to our fathers,
To Abraham, and to his seed for ever."

THE MANGER CRADLE

JOSEPH was busy in his carpenter shop, in the little town of Nazareth one day, when a messenger came to the door.

"Joseph," said the messenger, "the king has made a new law, that everyone must go back to his own home city, to be enrolled.

"You and Mary will both have to go to Bethlehem and enroll your names there, because Bethlehem was your old home."

Joseph, always ready to obey the king's commands, stopped his work and went to tell Mary the news.

It was a long trip for them to make. Mary had to ride on a donkey, while Joseph walked beside her.

They stopped to rest many times and at last after several days, Mary and Joseph reached the little town of Bethlehem. They went first to the inn, where travelers always stayed.

Joseph asked the inn-keeper for a room, but the inn-keeper shook his head.

"The inn is full," he said, "and I do not know where you can go. The whole town is filled with travelers."

[17]

Joseph and Mary hunted and hunted for a place to lay their heads, but they could find nothing but a stable. And at last they had to go there to sleep.

In the night—a little boy baby was born to Mary.

She wrapped Him in swaddling clothes and laid Him very gently in the manger.

Perhaps you have sung this song about the Baby of Bethlehem:

"Away in a manger, no crib for His bed,
The little Lord Jesus laid down His sweet head.
The stars in the sky looked down where He lay,
The little Lord Jesus asleep in the hay."

Now this was the same Mary, to whom an angel had come in the springtime, telling her that she would be the mother of a little boy baby and that she should call His name Jesus. It made her very happy, to know that the angel's promise had come true.

That night, out on the hillside, not far from Bethlehem, shepherds were keeping watch over their flocks. It was a fine, clear night and the stars were shining brightly, in the blue sky.

Suddenly a bright light, brighter than any star, shone round about them. The Bible says, "It was the glory of the Lord."

The shepherds were very much frightened, but in the light, an angel appeared saying, "Be not afraid. For behold, I bring you good tidings of great joy, which shall be to all people.

"For unto you is born this day, in the city of David, a Saviour which is Christ the Lord.

"And this shall be a sign unto you. Ye shall find the babe wrapped in swaddling clothes, lying in a manger."

And suddenly there appeared a host of angels praising God, and saying:

"Glory to God in the highest,
And on earth, peace, good will toward men."

As soon as the chorus was ended, the angels went back to heaven.

A BRIGHT LIGHT, BRIGHTER THAN ANY STAR, SHONE ROUND ABOUT THEM

The astonished shepherds said to one another, "Let us now go to Bethlehem and see the Baby."

They left their flocks and hurried to the town and there they found Mary and Joseph and the Baby.

They knelt beside the Baby lying asleep in the manger and worshipped Him. And as they looked at the Baby Jesus, they told Mary and Joseph about the angel in the bright light and what he had said about the Child.

They gave the good news to others too, that Jesus had really come and they went back to their flocks, praising and thanking God, for the wonderful thing that had happened.

THE BABY JESUS IN THE TEMPLE

WHEN the Baby Jesus was about forty days old, Mary and Joseph prepared to take Him to the temple and offer a sacrifice, according to the Jewish law.

So they started with the Baby, on the long trip to the temple.

As Mary and Joseph drew near, they saw a man outside of the temple selling doves.

In those days, when anyone felt very grateful to God for some special kindness, they bought doves and offered them as a sacrifice. It was a way of thanking God.

Mary and Joseph bought two doves and carried them with the Baby, into the temple.

On that day, an old man of Jerusalem, had come to the temple. His name was Simeon. He had been a very good man all his life and had tried his best to do right.

Often God had talked with Simeon and once He had said to him, "Some day, Simeon, you shall see Jesus."

When Simeon saw Joseph and Mary bringing the Child, he went to them and took the Baby in his arms.

Simeon was happier that moment than he had ever been in his life, because he knew that the Baby he was holding, was the Son of God.

He lifted his eyes to heaven while he held Jesus in his arms and spoke to God in prayer. This is what he said:

> "Lord, now lettest thou thy servant depart
> In peace, according to thy word.
> For mine eyes have seen thy salvation."

There was a good old woman in the temple that day, her name was Anna.

Anna was as glad to see the Son of God, as Simeon had been.

After awhile Mary and Joseph took the Baby home, leaving behind a happy old man and woman.

HE LIFTED HIS EYES TO HEAVEN WHILE HE HELD JESUS IN HIS ARMS

THE WISE MEN AND THE STAR IN THE EAST

LONG, long before the little Baby Jesus was born in Bethlehem, God had promised the people, that some day He would send His son to earth.

Just how God would send Him, they could not tell, but they did know, that He would keep His promise.

In a country far away from Bethlehem, there lived some good men called wise men, because they knew so much about many things.

These men sat under the stars every night and talked about these wonderful lights, that God had put in the sky. They taught the people about the stars, and of God's love and greatness.

These wise men had learned, that a new star would come to tell them, when God had sent His Son.

Night after night, they spoke of God's promise.

At last there came a night, when the most beautiful star they had ever seen, appeared in the sky. The wise men watching it, felt sure that this must be the special star, sent to tell them that God's Son was born.

This beautiful star appeared in the east on the very night, that

KING HEROD SENT FOR THE WISE MEN

the shepherds saw the wonderful light in the sky, as they watched their sheep.

The wise men, as well as the shepherds, wanted to go and worship the Son of God. They knew that God's Son was to be born in a country where His people, the Jews, lived. This was a long way from their own land. They must cross a hot, sandy desert to find the new-born Baby.

The wise men lost no time in making ready for the journey. There was only one way to cross the desert and that was on the backs of camels.

Fortunately the wise men owned many camels, for they were rich. They ordered their servants to load the camels with food, clothing and everything needed for a long, hard journey. Just before the start, the camels were given a good drink of water, a drink that would last them for many days, for there was no water in the desert.

The big, lumbering beasts dropped on their knees and waited for their burdens. Then came the wise men, dressed in their finest clothes of velvet and silk, each one carrying a gift for the Baby Jesus. When the precious packages were stowed away in the saddle bags and the wise men had climbed on the camels' backs, they set off.

The travelers looked up at the star. It seemed to say, "Come, follow me, and I will show you where to find the new-born King."

The wise men crossed the hot sands of the desert, and when at last they reached rivers and mountains, they knew they were drawing nearer to the country of the new King.

They came after a time to a great city, with high walls around it. They knew that this must be Jerusalem. The gatekeeper let them in, but he could tell them nothing about the new-born King.

How the people stared, as these strange visitors came riding through the streets!

"Where is He that is born King of the Jews?" the wise men asked over and over, as they rode along.

At last King Herod heard about these richly dressed strangers. It worried him to think they were looking for a new baby King.

He called some of the most important men of the city together, to find out what they knew about God's promise, to send Jesus.

"Where was the Christ to be born?" asked Herod. And the chief priests and scribes answered, "The prophet tells us, he would be born in Bethlehem."

Then King Herod sent for the wise men, to come to his palace. He asked them many questions, about the time the star appeared and he told them to go to Bethlehem and look for the Baby.

He asked them to come back to his palace and tell him about the Child; saying, "I, too, want to go to worship him."

The wise men had no sooner gone out of King Herod's palace and climbed on their camels, than they again saw the star, which they had seen in the far east, and it went on before them.

It led them on and on, to Bethlehem, and stood over the house, where Mary and Joseph and the Baby were.

Inside they found the Baby Jesus and His mother.

They fell down and worshipped Him, just as the shepherds had done, and they gave Him the costly gifts they had brought from home: gold, frankincense, and myrrh.

The wise men, had intended to go back to Herod's palace at Jerusalem, just as the King had asked them. But God in heaven was taking care of His Son. He sent the wise men a dream, to warn them not to return to King Herod's palace, but to go back home a different way, and they did this.

THE FLIGHT INTO EGYPT

HEROD, as you read in the last story, was king in Jerusalem, when the wise men came looking for Jesus. He said to them, "When you have found the new King, come back and let me know where He is, for I, too, want to worship Him."

But Herod did not really want to worship Jesus at all. He meant to harm Him.

"A new King," he complained. "*I* am the king myself, and this Baby shall not stand in my way."

After the wise men had found Jesus and given Him their precious gifts, a message came from God, directing them not to go home by way of Jerusalem and they heeded this message.

Now King Herod had thought that it would be the easiest thing in the world to get the Baby into His own hands, once the wise men had told him where He was.

It made him very angry, to hear they had not done as he ordered.

Day after day passed and still King Herod, learned nothing more about the Baby Jesus.

[28]

At last, he called his soldiers and sent them through the country, to kill all the little boy babies two years old, or younger.

Joseph and Mary did not know the danger that threatened the Baby Jesus, but the Father in Heaven knew and was watching over His Son.

One night when Mary and Joseph were asleep, He sent an angel to Joseph in a dream.

"Arise," said the angel softly, "and take the young child and his mother and flee into Egypt. Be thou there until I bring thee word; for Herod will seek the young child to destroy him."

Joseph wakened Mary and gave her the message.

"We must go at once," they said to each other, "to save Jesus from the wicked King."

Mary gathered together a few belongings and Joseph brought the donkey from the shed. Mary wrapped up the Baby and off they started for the land of Egypt.

Mary and Joseph stayed in Egypt a long time, until they learned that Herod, the old king, had died.

This was the way the message of his death came to Joseph:

One night as he was asleep, an angel appeared to him in a dream.

"Arise and take the young child and his mother and go into the land of Israel," said the angel. "For they are dead which sought the young child's life."

Again Joseph obeyed the Voice; he arose and took Jesus and Mary and started back to their old home. God told him in a dream just where to go, and he went into Galilee to the little town of Nazareth.

Joseph and Mary and Jesus lived happily in Nazareth, until God called Jesus to His great work.

THE VISIT TO JERUSALEM

"NOW his parents went to Jerusalem every year, at the feast of the passover.

And when he was twelve years old, they went up to Jerusalem, after the custom of the feast.

And when they had fulfilled the days, as they returned, the child Jesus tarried behind in Jerusalem; and Joseph and his mother knew not of it.

But they, supposing him to have been in the company, went a day's journey; and they sought him among their kinsfolk and acquaintance.

And when they found him not, they turned back again to Jerusalem, seeking him.

And it came to pass, that after three days, they found him in the temple, sitting in the midst of the doctors, both hearing them, and asking them questions.

And all that heard him, were astonished at his understanding and answers.

And when they saw him, they were amazed; and his mother said unto him, Son, why hast thou thus dealt with us? behold, thy father and I have sought thee sorrowing.

And he said unto them, 'How is it that ye sought me? Wist ye not that I must be about my Father's business?'

And they understood not the saying which he spake unto them.

And he went down with them, and came to Nazareth; and was subject unto them; but his mother kept all these sayings in her heart.

And Jesus increased in wisdom and stature; and in favor with God and man.''

JOHN THE BAPTIST AND JESUS

JESUS had a cousin called John. He was only six months old, when Jesus was born.

John's father and mother were very good people and they brought up their little boy carefully.

Now even before John was born, God had planned that he should be a preacher, to tell the people about His Son, Jesus, whom he would send to save the world.

When the boy, John, grew older he left his home and went out into the wilderness to live. His food was locusts and wild honey. He wore a garment made of camel's hair, with a leather belt around his waist.

In the wilderness he listened to God's voice and prayed to Him for guidance.

Then one day when John had grown to be a man, he knew that the time had come, for him to begin his work.

In his strange camel's hair garment and with a staff in his hand, he traveled through the country along the River Jordan. He urged the people to be baptized, to show they were sorry for their sins and wished to be forgiven.

As he traveled along the river bank he called again and again, "Prepare ye the way of the Lord; make His paths straight."

Those who were really sorry for their sins, he baptized in the River Jordan.

Crowds of people listened to the preaching of John the Baptist, and watched him baptize those who were sorry for their sins.

Many from the crowd asked John:

"What must we do?"

John said: "If you have two coats and find some one who has none, give him one; if you have food to eat and your neighbor has none, give him some of yours."

The tax-gatherers came to John and asked what they ought to do, and John answered: "Don't take a cent more than is due you."

HE LEFT HIS HOME AND WENT OUT INTO THE WILDERNESS

And the soldiers came and said: "What must we do?" John said: "Do no violence to any one, and be content with your wages."

As they listened to John's words, the people wondered if he might not be Christ himself, but John said to them: "There cometh one mightier than I after me, the latchet of whose shoes, I am not worthy to stoop down and unloose."

One day while John was baptizing in the Jordan River, Jesus came from His far-away home. He stepped out into the river and asked John to baptize Him. At first John did not want to. He said, "Jesus, I have need to be baptized of thee."

But Jesus answered him very gently, saying: "John, suffer it to be so now, for thus it becometh us to fulfil all righteousness."

Then John baptized Jesus. And as they came up out of the water, the heavens were opened, and the Spirit of God, in the form of a dove, came down over Jesus' head, and a voice from heaven said: "This is my beloved Son, in whom I am well pleased."

JESUS AND THE NOBLEMAN'S SON

A VERY rich nobleman, lived in the city of Capernaum. He had a little son, whom he loved very dearly. One day the boy became ill. The best doctors in the city of Capernaum were called, but they could not help him. It looked as if the little boy would never get well.

The nobleman could not bear to think of losing his dear child. How could he save him?

Then he heard one day, that there was a Man in the town, who could do wonderful things; he had even made blind eyes see again.

"Surely," said the nobleman, "he can help my child."

At once he decided to find Jesus and ask him to come to his house.

Jesus spent much of the time in Capernaum, where the nobleman lived, but it happened on this day, that He was in the city of Cana, twenty miles away.

Now twenty miles on a donkey, on horseback or on a camel, is a hard journey, but the anxious father cared nothing for that.

[35]

Taking some of his servants, he started at once for Cana; he would let no one go in his place.

Perhaps he wanted to show Jesus, that he really believed, He could heal his son.

At last the nobleman reached Cana and found Jesus busy at His work. He begged Him to go back to Capernaum and heal his boy, who was lying at the point of death.

Jesus looked at the richly dressed man; He looked at his bodyguard, and then He asked a question, to make sure that the man was in earnest.

The nobleman's answer was, "Sir, come down before my child dies."

The good kind Master knew how anxious the father would be on the long journey back to Capernaum. So He turned to the man and said, "Go thy way; thy son liveth."

The nobleman set out for home joyfully, for he believed all that Jesus had said to him, that he would find his boy cured.

As he went along, some of his servants from home, came out to meet him.

They came bringing the good news: "Your son is better."

"When did he begin to feel better?" the happy father asked eagerly.

"Yesterday about the seventh hour," the servants told him. That was the same as saying, "Yesterday about one o'clock."

Then the father knew, that was the very time, when Jesus had said to him, "Thy son liveth."

He hurried home to see his dear son. There was joy indeed in the nobleman's house that day and there were hearts grateful to Jesus, who had made the boy well.

Ever after that the nobleman and his whole household, were the staunch friends of Jesus.

HEALING THE CRIPPLE AT BETHESDA

IN the city of Jerusalem there was a pool, called the Pool of Bethesda. The pool had five porches. These porches were always crowded with people, the sick, the blind and the lame.

They came there filled with hope, for at certain times of the year, an angel went down into the pool and stirred the waters. Then the first one to step in, was cured of his illness.

It was no wonder that people gathered at the pool and waited patiently, for the angel to come. It was no wonder that each hoped, he would be the first to step into the waters.

Among those who went day after day, was a man who had been sick for thirty-eight years. Each time he went there was great hope in his heart, that he would be the first to get into the troubled waters.

He had seen the water bubble many times, but there was no one to help him and he was too crippled, to get into the pool by himself.

One day Jesus passed that way and saw the sick man lying on his mattress, inside one of the five porches. He knew that he had been waiting a long time.

Jesus stopped to talk to the man.

"Wilt thou be made whole?" He asked.

The cripple answered, "Sir, I have no man, when the water is troubled, to put me into the pool: but while I am coming, another steppeth down before me."

Jesus said to him, "Rise, take up thy bed and walk."

And the man who had been lying helpless so long, took up his bed and walked!

JESUS CAME DOWN TO THE SHORE OF THE LAKE OF GALILEE

JESUS AND THE FISHERMEN

ONE day, Jesus came down to the shore of the Lake of Galilee, followed by crowds of people, eager to listen to his words.

There were two empty boats by the shore and Jesus stepped into one, that belonged to Simon Peter. He sat down in the boat and spoke to the great crowds on the shore.

When Jesus stopped speaking, He turned to Simon Peter and said, "Launch out into the deep and let down your nets for a draught."

But Simon answered, "Master, we have toiled all night, and have taken nothing; nevertheless at thy word, I will let down the net."

As soon as they let the net down into the water, it was filled with fish, so many that the net broke.

Simon and his brother could not manage the net by themselves. They had to call their partners, James and John, who were in another boat near by.

James and John brought their boat close to Simon's, and the men worked quickly, so as not to lose any of the fish.

Soon both boats were so full, that they began to sink.

Simon Peter was badly frightened. He fell down at Jesus' knees and cried out, "Leave me, Lord, for I am a sinful man."

He meant that he did not deserve to be with anyone so good.

James and John and Andrew felt just as Simon Peter did, but Jesus, in his kind, gentle way said to them:

"Fear not, from henceforth thou shalt catch men."

And as soon as the men brought their boats to land, they left everything and followed Jesus.

Ever after that Simon Peter and Andrew, his brother, James and John, the sons of Zebedee, were among Jesus' loved disciples.

THE SERMON ON THE MOUNT

AS the news spread of the wonderful things Jesus did, people came from far and near to hear Him and they brought their sick to be healed.

The disciples whom He had chosen, stayed close by to learn from their beloved Master.

They wondered, as they saw Him heal the sick, make blind eyes see and deaf ears hear. The crowds wondered, too, at His power. And they loved Him for his gentleness and kindness.

Wherever Jesus went they followed and it was hard for Him, to get even a moment's rest.

One day He led them up a mountainside. He sat down on its slope and His disciples gathered about Him. The people clustered close, to catch every word from His lips.

There were many things that Jesus wanted His followers to remember. Some of these things, He told them that day in a great sermon, the greatest sermon the world has ever known, called the "Sermon on the Mount."

Here are some of the beautiful things He said:

"Blessed are the poor in spirit; for their's is the kingdom of heaven.

Blessed are they that mourn: for they shall be comforted.

Blessed are the meek: for they shall inherit the earth.

Blessed are they which do hunger and thirst after righteousness: for they shall be filled.

Blessed are the merciful: for they shall obtain mercy.

Blessed are the pure in heart: for they shall see God.

Blessed are the peacemakers: for they shall be called the children of God.

Blessed are they which are persecuted for righteousness' sake: for their's is the kingdom of heaven.

Blessed are ye, when men shall revile you, and persecute you, and shall say all manner of evil against you falsely, for my sake.

Rejoice, and be exceeding glad: for great is your reward in heaven: for so persecuted they the prophets which were before you."

The Beatitudes, Matt: 5: 3-12.

"But I say unto you which hear, Love your enemies, do good to them which hate you, bless them that curse you, and pray for them which despitefully use you.

And unto him that smiteth thee on the one cheek offer also the other; and him that taketh away thy cloke forbid not to take thy coat also.

Give to every man that asketh of thee; and of him that taketh away thy goods ask them not again.

And as ye would that men should do to you, do ye also to them likewise.

For if ye love them which love you, what thank have ye? for sinners also love those that love them.

And if ye do good to them which do good to you, what thank have ye? for sinners also do even the same.

And if ye lend to them of whom ye hope to receive, what thank have ye? for sinners also lend to sinners, to receive as much again.

But love ye your enemies, and do good, and lend, hoping for nothing again; and your reward shall be great, and ye shall be the children of the Highest: for he is kind unto the unthankful and to the evil.

Be ye therefore merciful, as your Father also is merciful.

Judge not, and ye shall not be judged: condemn not, and ye shall not be condemned: forgive, and ye shall be forgiven:

Give, and it shall be given unto you: good measure, pressed down, and shaken together, and running over, shall men give into your bosom. For with the same measure that ye mete withal it shall be measured to you again."

Luke 6: 27-38.

WHAT JESUS TAUGHT ABOUT PRAYER

MANY times when Jesus and His disciples were together, He would leave them for just a little while and go to a quiet place to pray.

His disciples often wished that they might pray just as He did. One day after Jesus had come back from His quiet prayer one of them said to Him, "Lord, teach us to pray." And Jesus was glad to teach them.

He told them that they should talk to the Father in heaven, and the very first words that He used were words of praise to the heavenly Father.

He told them that they should ask for the things which they needed, and that the Father in heaven would always answer their prayers, in the very best ways for them.

He said to them, "After this manner, therefore, pray ye."

>Our Father which art in Heaven
>Hallowed be thy name.
>Thy kingdom come, thy will be done,
>In earth as it is in Heaven,
>Give us this day, our daily bread.
>And forgive us our debts
>As we forgive our debtors.
>And lead us not into temptation;
>But deliver us from evil.
>For thine is the Kingdom,
>And the power,
>And the glory forever.

Jesus so much wanted his disciples to understand the great love of the Father in heaven and how willing He is to answer their prayers.

He made it clear to them that they might pray at any time and in any place and that God would always listen and answer.

"Ask and ye shall receive," said Jesus, "seek and ye shall find, knock and it shall be opened unto you, for every one that asketh, receiveth and he that seeketh findeth, and to him that knocketh, it shall be opened.

"When your child asks something good will you give him something evil?

"If he asks for bread will you give him a stone? If he asks for fish will you give him a serpent?"

And then He added, "If you know how to give good gifts to your children, how much more does your heavenly Father know how to give good gifts to you."

Jesus one time told His disciples the story about two men who went up to the temple to pray. One of these men was a very rich Pharisee, and the other was a poor publican.

The proud rich Pharisee threw back his head and said "God, I thank Thee that I am not as the rest of men. I'm better than most men. I thank Thee that I'm not like this publican. I fast twice a week and I give tithes of all I get."

The poor publican was not proud. He was humble. He knew that he was not better than other people and he didn't pretend that he was.

He bowed his head very meekly and said, "Oh, God, be merciful to me a sinner." Then he asked the Father in Heaven to forgive all the wrongs he had done.

"This man rather than the other prayed aright," said Jesus.

One other very important thing that Jesus said to His disciples was this: "Do not pray just to be seen and heard of men, but go into your closet and pray to your Father in secret, and your Father which seeth in secret himself shall reward you openly."

You can pray anywhere anytime that you want to, but Jesus meant that you should go to a quiet place where you could talk to God about everything; tell Him your needs, and ask His help, and you may be sure He will listen, and if you pray for the right things He will answer your prayer.

"God make my life a little light
　　Within this world to glow,
　A little flame that burneth bright
　　Wherever I may go."

THE TWELVE APOSTLES

JESUS was filled with pity, for the people who thronged to hear his preaching and be cured of their ills. They seemed to Him like a great flock of sheep, without a shepherd to guide them.

Every day he talked to them and healed their sicknesses.

He had chosen four men, you will remember, to help Him in His work. Afterwards he asked eight more men to help Him.

These are the names of the twelve disciples:

The first, Simon, who is called Peter, and Andrew, his brother; James, the son of Zebedee, and John his brother;

"Philip, and Bartholomew; Thomas, and Matthew the publican; James, the son of Alphaeus, and Lebbaeus, whose surname was Thaddaeus;

Simon, the Canaanite, and Judas Iscariot, who also betrayed Him."

These twelve disciples had been learning from Jesus, how to help people in trouble.

One day He called them together and told them to go forth and preach, telling everyone, "The kingdom of heaven is at hand."

He gave them power over evil spirits, and said to them, "Heal the sick, cleanse the lepers, raise the dead, cast out devils: freely ye have received, freely give."

It was Jesus' dearest wish, that His disciples should help people, to be good and happy and well.

Jesus told His twelve helpers to take no money with them, no extra clothing, not even anything to eat. He knew that they would be cared for, by the people they helped.

He told them, too, that some would be sure to speak evil of them, and they might be put in prison, but that they should not fear, for the Father in heaven would be watching over them and caring for them.

He reminded them that sparrows are tiny creatures, worth very little, but that not one could fall to the ground, without the Father knowing it.

"The very hairs of your head are numbered," said Jesus. "Fear not ye therefore, ye are of more value than many sparrows."

After Jesus had finished telling His disciples, just what they should do, they set out to begin their work, and He went away to teach and to preach in other places.

THE WIDOW'S SON

ONE day Jesus was traveling to a city called Nain. His disciples were with Him, and, as usual, a great crowd followed.

As they drew near the city gate, they saw a funeral coming and were told that it was a young man, a poor widow's only son, who had died.

When Jesus saw the grieving mother, he was very sorry for her. "Weep not," He said to her gently.

He touched the stretcher, on which her son's body lay and the men who were carrying it stood still.

Then Jesus said, "Young man, I say unto thee, arise."

Everybody looked on in wonder, as the young man sat up and began to speak. Jesus took him by the hand and gave him back to his mother, and all her sorrow was changed to joy.

The bystanders all glorified God, saying, "A great prophet is arisen among us: and, God hath visited his people."

THEN JESUS SAID, "YOUNG MAN, I SAY UNTO THEE, ARISE."

PEACE, BE STILL

IN the country where Jesus lived, there is a beautiful little lake, the lake of Galilee.

Sometimes it is called the Sea of Galilee.

Jesus liked to walk along the shore of this lake, and often when He was tired, He would go out in a boat on its quiet waters.

One evening after Jesus had been teaching and healing the sick all day, and had been followed by even greater crowds than usual, He asked some of his disciples to go with Him, across to the other side of the lake.

They had no more than pulled away from the shore, when Jesus, who was sitting in the stern of the boat, fell asleep.

Suddenly a storm came up. The wind blew hard and the waves dashed high. The water was beginning to fill the boat.

The disciples were very much frightened, but Jesus slept on.

At last they were so afraid, that they woke Jesus, asking Him if He did not care if they were all lost.

"Master, carest thou not that we perish?" they cried.

Jesus opened His eyes and saw their anxious, frightened faces.

He stood up in the boat and spoke to the stormy winds and to the angry sea.

"Peace, be still," He said in His gentle tones.

At once the wind stopped blowing. The waves no longer dashed over the boat. The storm was over.

Jesus asked the disciples why they were afraid and why they had not more faith.

The men were amazed, at what they had just seen Jesus do.

They knew that He could cure all kinds of disease. They had seen Him cleanse the leper; they had seen Him make crooked legs stand straight; they had seen Him give sight to the blind. They had seen Him raise the dead.

And now they had seen Him calm the storm!

"What manner of man is this," they cried, "that even the wind and the sea obey Him?"

They felt, that they could sail on forever with Him.

THE RULER'S DAUGHTER

IN the far away country where Jesus lived, there was a very rich man, whose name was Jairus.

Jairus was an important man in his city. He was a ruler of the synagogue.

Jairus and his wife had just one child, a little girl twelve years old. It was a sad day for them, when this little daughter became ill.

They did everything they could for her, but she grew steadily worse.

At last Jairus said, "I will ask Jesus to come; He has helped many people and I am sure He will come here and make her well."

Jairus found Jesus busy healing the sick and preaching. He pushed his way through the crowds and fell at His feet. "My little daughter is at the point of death!" he cried. "I pray thee come and lay thy hands upon her, that she may be healed and live."

Jesus started with him at once and the crowds followed.

There were so many people begging to be healed, that He stopped and helped some of them.

As He was talking to a woman whom He had just cured of a long illness, a messenger came to Jairus, saying, "Thy daughter is dead. Trouble not the Master."

It was a hard moment for Jairus, but Jesus turned to him and said, "Fear not, believe only."

Then Jesus took Peter and James and John and went to Jairus' home.

A sad sight met their eyes! The house was filled with people, sobbing and crying.

Jesus said to the mourners. "Why do you weep and make this noise? The child is not dead but sleepeth."

The mourners thought Jesus did not understand what had really happened, and made light of what He said.

Jesus asked them to go outside. Then with only Peter, James and John and the father and mother of the little girl, He went into the room where she was lying.

It was very hard for the father and mother to look at their little child, now white and still.

Jesus was very sorry for them, but He did not weep. He took the little girl by the hand, saying:

"Damsel, I say unto thee, arise."

And that very moment, the little girl stood up and walked about. Jesus told her father and mother to give her something to eat.

The home of Jairus was the happiest one in the city of Capernaum that day.

And Jairus and his wife never forgot to be grateful to Jesus, for giving their dear little daughter back to them.

FEEDING THE FIVE THOUSAND

THERE was once a little boy, who lived with his mother, near the Sea of Galilee. This boy had heard of Jesus and of the strange things He did and he was eager to see this wonderful Man.

"Will you let me go to see Jesus?" he asked his mother one day.

"Yes, son," said the mother, "if you will be careful not to get hurt."

"I will be careful, mother," he promised.

His mother knew that boys are always hungry, so she packed a lunch for him. It was very small—only five small barley cakes and two dried fish.

The boy took his little basket of food and soon found himself among the great crowd following Jesus. He followed along, too, and all through the day watched Jesus as He healed the sick.

Now after a time Jesus' helpers reminded Him that it was growing late, and that the people ought to go away to get something to eat.

Jesus told His disciples not to send them away, but to feed them there.

The disciples began to look for food among the crowd, but they found only one person who had any and that was our little boy.

Andrew came back to Jesus with the word, "There is a little boy here, who has five barley loaves and two fishes."

Jesus said, "Bring them to me," and Andrew told the boy, that Jesus had asked for his food.

The boy went with Andrew to Jesus' side and gladly gave Him what he had.

He did not know what a strange thing was to happen, to his five small loaves and two fishes.

Jesus asked His helpers to tell the people to sit down on the grass, in groups of fifty and one hundred.

Then He took the loaves and fishes and looked up to heaven and thanked God for all His good gifts.

He blessed the loaves and broke them and His helpers passed the food to the great crowd.

As Jesus broke the five loaves, there were more and more!

And as the helpers passed the food to the crowd, there was more and more of it!

Every one in all that great crowd had all he could eat, and there were five thousand men, besides the women and children!

After the meal was over, Jesus said, "Gather up all the pieces that nothing be lost."

And they gathered up *twelve* baskets full of pieces!

How happy the boy of Galilee was, that he had helped Jesus!

THEN JESUS TOOK THE LOAVES AND FISHES

JESUS WALKING ON THE WATER

ON the day that Jesus had fed the great multitude, with the little boy's five loaves and two small fishes, the people wanted to make Him king.

But Jesus was not willing. He asked them to go to their homes and He sent His disciples for a boat, to cross the Sea of Galilee to Capernaum.

Then He went up on a mountain to pray, and He stayed there alone in the darkness.

Meanwhile the disciples were on their way across the lake. The wind was against them and their boat tossed about in the waves.

Suddenly the disciples looked up and saw a figure walking on the water.

"It is a Spirit," they cried out in fear.

Then they heard the voice of Jesus saying, "Be of good cheer; it is I; be not afraid."

"Lord, if it be thou, bid me come to thee on the water," Peter cried out.

"Come," said Jesus.

Then Peter stepped out of the boat and began to walk on the water toward Jesus.

At first he had no fear, but as the wind blew wildly about him, he lost courage.

"Lord, save me," cried Peter as he began to sink in the water. Immediately Jesus stretched out His hand and caught him; then He said, "O Peter, why didn't you have more faith? Why did you doubt?"

Jesus and Peter got into the boat. The wind stopped blowing— and the sea grew calm.

The disciples who had seen Jesus do this marvelous thing, worshipped Him and there was no doubt in their minds, that He was God's own Son.

JESUS MAKES A BLIND MAN SEE

"POOR little baby!" said a young mother, as she looked into the round, chubby face of her baby boy.

"Poor little blind boy! He will never, never see," and again she looked at the great dark eyes, that seemed to be covered with a heavy veil.

It was very hard for the mother and father to know that their baby would never see the beautiful things around him.

He could never see his dear mother's face, nor his daddy's kind eyes.

As the little boy grew older, how he must have wished, that he could see the sunshine, the birds, and the flowers.

His mother and father tried in vain, to get help for the poor blind eyes, and the child grew to manhood—blind.

In those days, the blind had not been taught how to work and earn a living. This poor man had to beg for everything that he had.

Almost every day he sat by the roadside, where the people were coming and going and reached out his hand for help.

HE DIPPED THE WATER UP IN HIS HANDS AND WASHED HIS EYES

One day Jesus passed by and saw the man. His gentle heart was moved with pity.

Some of His friends were with Him and Jesus wanted them to know about God's power.

He stepped quickly to the blind man's side and spat on the ground; then He stooped down, mixed a little clay with His fingers and put it on the blind eyes.

The touch of Jesus' fingers was very gentle and soothing to the poor eyes.

"Go to the pool of Siloam," said the great Teacher, "and wash in it."

The blind man hurried to the pool. He dipped the water up in his hands and washed his eyes.

He opened them—he could see!

As he was going home someone said, "Isn't this the blind beggar, that sat by the wayside?" "Yes, it is he," said another. And still another said, "No, it isn't he. It looks like him, but it isn't."

The blind man turned to them saying, "I am he."

Everybody crowded around him, asking how it happened that he could see, and he told them just what Jesus had said and done.

He told them how Jesus had mixed the clay and put it on his eyes, and that just as soon as he washed it off, he could see.

And this man, who had never before seen the light of day, believed in Jesus and worshipped Him.

THE TRANSFIGURATION

AFTER Jesus had been on the earth for a long time, He had done many beautiful things for people. The Father in heaven wanted Jesus' close friends to understand how pleased He was and one day a very lovely thing happened.

Jesus took Peter, James and John and went up on the mountainside to pray. These three disciples were very tired; the Bible says: "They were heavy with sleep."

While Jesus was praying, suddenly His face became bright and shining and His garments became white and glistering.

The Bible says, "His face did shine like the sun and His garments became white as the light."

The three disciples were startled. While they were watching, two of God's great helpers of the long ago, Moses and Elijah, came out of heaven and took their places on either side of Jesus.

Moses and Elijah long before, had worked very hard to get all of the people to live as God wanted them to do.

Peter, James and John had been with Jesus much of the time, but they had never seen anything as wonderful as Jesus' shining face and the whiteness of His garments.

[63]

These disciples had never seen anything so strange as two men, who had lived so long ago, come down from heaven and stand by Jesus.

They were glad that Jesus had taken them up on the mountainside with Him; and that they had seen His glory.

Peter was so glad that he spoke out: "Master, it is good for us to be here; and let us make three tabernacles; one for Thee, one for Moses and one for Elijah."

Even as Peter spoke a bright cloud came floating over them and the men were afraid.

But out of the cloud there came a voice. It was the voice of God saying: "This is my Beloved Son; hear ye Him."

When the men lifted their eyes and looked around, "they saw no man any more, save Jesus only with themselves."

When the disciples came down from the mountainside, they thought and thought about the things which they had seen.

It had all been so very wonderful, the kind face of the loving Jesus, made even more beautiful than it had ever been before and His garments so white and dazzling.

They thought too, of the great workers, Moses and Elijah, who had stood on the mountain by Jesus.

Very tenderly they thought of God's voice saying to them: "This is my Beloved Son; hear ye Him."

And the Bible says they held their peace.

THE GOOD SHEPHERD

ONCE there was a good shepherd, who had a hundred sheep. He knew every one of them by name.

The sheep loved their shepherd and they would come at his call.

The good shepherd tried always, to lead his sheep into green pastures and beside cool streams.

All day they followed him over the hills, grazing or resting in the shade.

In the evening, the shepherd called his sheep and slowly they would go down over the hills and fields, until they came to the sheepfold.

At the door of the fold, the shepherd stopped and held up the rod he carried all day, until the sheep one by one went in.

As they went past the shepherd he counted them. If even one sheep was missing, the shepherd took no rest until it was found.

One day on the hillside a little lamb strayed away from the flock. He nibbled the grass, here and there, until he had strayed so far, he couldn't find his way back.

THE SHEPHERD WAS GLAD TO FIND THE SHEEP THAT WAS LOST

At evening, the shepherd called his sheep and led them home to the fold. He counted—"one, two, three," and on up to "ninety-seven, ninety-eight and ninety-nine," but there was not one hundred. There were only ninety-nine. The shepherd knew that one sheep was missing!

Night was coming on and it was dark and rainy, but the shepherd started out, without a thought of the storm. He went along calling the little lamb's name, but no little lamb gave an answering "Baa."

He went on and on, calling all the time, for he knew that if the little lamb heard his name, he would come running.

At last, the tired shepherd heard a faint little "Baa, baa."

Then he knew, that his little lost lamb was answering him.

The shepherd got down on his knees and crept toward the spot from which the sound came. He tore his hands on the thorns, until they were bleeding. He reached out and at last he touched the little woolly head. It was caught in the thorns, but the good shepherd tore them away and rescued his little lost lamb.

The shepherd was so glad to find the sheep that was lost, that he called in his neighbors, to rejoice with him.

Jesus told this story to the people, so that they would understand, just how dear every man and woman and little child is, to the Father in heaven.

He loves and cares for us tenderly, just as the good shepherd cared for his sheep.

"I am the Good Shepherd," said Jesus.

"My sheep know my voice."

"The Good Shepherd giveth His life for his sheep."

JESUS BLESSES LITTLE CHILDREN

IN the country where Jesus lived, there were many children and they were just like children everywhere else. They had bright eyes, to see what was going on and sharp ears to hear what was being said.

They played and romped as children do today. Sometimes they climbed the stairways of their cottages and said their prayers, on the flat roof tops.

The boys and girls in one little village, were very much excited one day, when they found that Jesus was coming to their town. They had heard their older brothers and sisters and their fathers and mothers, tell of the Man who had brought a little girl to life. He had made blind men see and lame men walk and had cured many sick people. They were very eager to see Him.

The fathers and mothers were happy, too, that Jesus was coming. They began to plan at once to take their children, where He could see them. They wanted the Master to lay His loving hands on their little ones.

You may be sure, these mothers did their best, to make their little folks clean and tidy for this wonderful visit. At last everybody was ready; they trudged along the road, fathers, mothers and little folks, all on their way to see Jesus.

When they came upon Him, He was very busy healing sick people, who had been brought to Him and telling how life could be made beautiful and right.

The fathers and mothers made their way through the crowd and held out the babies for Him to touch. The disciples who were helping Jesus, tried to keep them back. They feared that these little ones would disturb the Master in His work, with the grown people.

But Jesus saw the disappointed faces of the mothers and fathers and children. Turning to the disciples He said:

"Suffer little children to come unto Me, and forbid them not; for of such is the kingdom of heaven."

"SUFFER LITTLE CHILDREN TO COME UNTO ME"

The disciples had been mistaken. Jesus loved the little children, too much to send them away. He took them in His arms and laid His hands on them and blessed them.

All through their lives, these little children were to remember that wonderful day, when the Master had held them in His arms and taught the world that:

"Whosoever shall not receive the kingdom of God, as a little child, shall in no wise enter therein."

THE RICH YOUNG RULER

A RICHLY dressed young man ran up to Jesus one day and flung himself on his knees at Jesus' feet.

"Good Master," he cried, "what shall I do, that I may inherit eternal life?"

The young man looked eagerly into the face of Jesus, and Jesus knew that he was very much in earnest.

"Why do you call me good?" asked Jesus. "There is none good save one, that is God."

Jesus told the young man to obey all the commandments: "Do not steal, or kill; keep thy life pure; honor thy father and mother; do not lie or cheat."

And the young man looking straight into Jesus' eyes, said quietly that he had kept all these commandments, ever since he had been a little boy.

Jesus felt a great liking for this young man.

He knew that the young man spoke the truth and that he had tried to do right, yet He said to him, "One thing thou lackest. Go, sell what thou hast and give to the poor, and thou shalt have treasure in heaven. And come, follow Me."

The young man was sorry to hear Jesus say this. He was very rich and he did not want to give up all the fine things, that made life pleasant. He thought he had done enough, by keeping the commandments. He went sadly away.

Jesus, turning to His disciples said, "How hard it is for those that trust in riches, to enter into the kingdom of God!"

The Bible does not tell us, whether or not, the young ruler ever came back to Jesus and did what He asked.

ZACCHAEUS—A MAN WHO WAS SORRY

IN the city of Jericho, there lived a rich man called Zacchaeus. He was a tax collector and he often took more money from the people, than was right.

One day Jesus passed through the city of Jericho, on His way to Jerusalem. As usual, great crowds of people gathered to see Him. Like everybody else, Zacchaeus wanted to get a glimpse of Jesus; but he was a very short man and could not see, over the heads of the crowd.

Zacchaeus could find nothing to stand on and he wondered what he would do. Then all of a sudden he had a happy thought. There was a sycamore tree further along the road. Zacchaeus ran ahead and climbed up into the branches, to watch for Jesus and the crowd to pass.

Something very surprising happened to the little man, waiting in the sycamore tree.

As Jesus passed by, He looked up. He saw Zacchaeus and spoke his name.

"Zacchaeus," said He, "make haste and come down, for today I must abide at thy house."

Zacchaeus felt very much honored, that Jesus had called him by name and had asked to come to his house.

He climbed down the tree, as fast as he could and welcomed Jesus joyfully.

Some of the bystanders were displeased, that Jesus should go to the home of a man, who had done wrong so often.

Jesus knew that Zacchaeus had not always been a good man, He knew, too, that from that day on, the tax-collector would never ask for a penny more, than was right.

Jesus knew that Zacchaeus, with His help, was going to try to be a better man.

That was the happiest day of Zacchaeus' life. He had found a Friend, who would help him to be honest and true.

He made this promise to the kind Teacher, who had come to his home, for rest and food:

"Lord, the half of my goods I will give to the poor, and if I have ever taken more than I should from any man, I will give him back four times as much as I took."

MARY AND MARTHA

JESUS had some very dear friends, in the little village of Bethany, a few miles away from Jerusalem.

He often went to visit them there. He knew He was always welcome in the home of Mary, Martha and their brother Lazarus.

On one of Jesus' visits, Martha was busying herself about the house, preparing good things for their Guest.

Mary, her sister, sat at the feet of Jesus, listening eagerly to His words.

After a time, Martha, tired of having all the work to do, came to Jesus and said, "Lord, dost thou not care that my sister hath left me to serve alone? Bid her, therefore, that she help me."

Jesus looked up at Martha and answered, "Martha, Martha, thou art careful and troubled about many things; but one thing is needful; and Mary hath chosen that good part which shall not be taken away from her."

JESUS BRINGS LAZARUS BACK TO LIFE

WHILE Jesus was away on a long journey, a great sorrow came to Mary and Martha in Bethany. Their brother Lazarus became ill and died. The two sisters longed to have Jesus come and comfort them in their trouble.

At last Jesus did come and Martha went out to meet Him.

"O Lord," she cried out to Him, "if thou hadst been here, my brother had not died." Then she hurried back to tell Mary that Jesus had come.

Mary's first words to Jesus, were the same as her sister's: "Lord, if thou hadst been here, my brother had not died."

Jesus was so sorry that He wept.

Then Jesus with Mary and Martha and the friends who had come to comfort them, went to the place where Lazarus had been buried.

Jesus cried out in a loud voice, "Lazarus, come forth." And Lazarus came out of the tomb, well and strong!

No wonder that Mary and Martha loved Jesus!

MARY POURED THE SWEET OINTMENT UPON HIS FEET

MARY'S GIFT TO JESUS

THE last week that Jesus was on earth, He spent some of His time with these three friends, Mary, Martha and Lazarus.

One evening they were at supper, with others of Jesus' dearest friends. Martha was busy, seeing that every one was well served.

In the midst of the meal, Mary very quietly left the room. A few moments later she came back, carrying a box of costly ointment. She had saved money enough to buy a whole pound of it and she wanted to give it all to Jesus.

She went to His side and poured the sweet ointment upon His feet and wiped them with her soft dark hair. The whole house was filled with the sweet scent of the ointment.

Judas, one of the disciples, spoke up complaining, "Why was not this ointment sold for three hundred pence and given to the poor?"

Mary made no answer, but Jesus knew what was in her heart.

"Do not trouble her," He said, "I shall not be with you very long, and Mary has done all she could for me. She hath wrought a good work on me.

"Verily I say unto you, wheresoever this gospel shall be preached throughout the whole world, this also that she hath done shall be spoken of for a memorial of her."

THE TRIUMPHAL ENTRY

AND it came to pass, when he was come nigh to Bethphage and Bethany, at the mount called the mount of Olives, he sent two of his disciples,

Saying, Go ye into the village over against you; in the which at your entering ye shall find a colt tied, whereon yet never man sat: loose him, and bring him hither.

And if any man ask you, Why do ye loose him? thus shall ye say unto him, Because the Lord hath need of him.

And they that were sent went their way, and found even as he had said unto them.

And as they were loosing the colt, the owners thereof said unto them, Why loose ye the colt?

And they said, The Lord hath need of him.

And they brought him to Jesus: and they cast their garments upon the colt, and they set Jesus thereon.

And as he went, they spread their clothes in the way.

And when he was come nigh, even now at the descent of the mount of Olives, the whole multitude of the disciples began to rejoice and praise God with a loud voice for all the mighty works that they had seen;

Saying, Blessed be the King that cometh in the name of the Lord: peace in heaven, and glory in the highest.

Luke 19: 29–38

THE GOOD SAMARITAN

ONE day while Jesus was on earth, shortly before He was crucified, some men were asking Him very hard questions—at least they thought they were hard.

Finally one of these men said to Jesus, "What is the greatest commandment in the law?" And Jesus answered: "Thou shalt love the Lord thy God with all thy heart, and with all thy soul, and with all thy mind and with all thy strength. This is the great and first commandment, And a second like unto it is this, Thou shalt love thy neighbor as thyself."

Don't you think that was a beautiful answer for Jesus to make?

Jesus had told the people many times, that they should love their neighbors as much as they loved themselves. That they should be willing to do for their neighbors, whatever they would do for themselves.

One of the men who were asking questions said to Him, "Lord, who is my neighbor?" And in order to make the man understand very clearly what He meant, Jesus told him a story.

It is called the story of the "Good Samaritan" and you can find it in your Bible in the gospel of St. Luke the 10th chapter. Here is the story:

One day there was a man in the city of Jerusalem, who was going to take a long journey to a city called Jericho.

The trip to Jericho was a very rough one—the road was rough and hilly. It was rough in another way too; oftentimes robbers would hide themselves in the caves along the road, or by the rocks and watch for travelers.

They would stop these travelers and take all their money or jewels or anything they had.

When the man whom Jesus told about, went from the city of Jerusalem to Jericho, some robbers were hidden by the rocks along the road. And when the man came along these robbers jumped from their hiding places and attacked him. They took all his money and beat him and hurt him very badly. They stripped his clothing off and left him half dead by the roadside.

The poor man lay there and after a long while, an officer of the church came by. He saw the man but he did not stop. He just drew his robes about him and passed by without offering to help him.

A second man came by. He, too, was an officer in the church, and he did not stop to help the poor man who had been beaten and hurt. He passed by and left the man lying there.

As the man lay on the ground presently he heard someone else coming; maybe he thought this one would not help him either, maybe he thought, "Oh it is no use to expect anyone to help me. I must just lie here and die."

But this time something happened, when this man came by he said, "Oh there is somebody that is hurt; he needs my help and I must stop and help him."

This third man who came along was called a Samaritan, because he came from a different country. The man who was hurt was from Jerusalem; he was a Jew. The one who stopped to help him was from Samaria; he was a Samaritan. The people of Jerusalem were not very good friends of the people of Samaria.

But the good Samaritan did not say, "I will not help that man because he comes from Jerusalem." He said, "There is somebody who is hurt; he needs my help and I must run and help him." He got right down from his donkey and went over to the man. He tore off his own garment and bound up the man's wounds. He poured oil on them so they would get well. Then he helped the man to his donkey and took him along the road until he came to an inn.

The good Samaritan gave the inn keeper some money and then he said, "Take care of this man, and if you spend more money than I have given you, when I come back this way I will repay you."

After Jesus had told this story he turned to the man who had asked the question, and said, "Which of these three men do you think was this poor man's neighbor?"

And the man answered, "He that showed mercy on him."

JUDAS BETRAYS JESUS

AMONG the disciples of Jesus, there was one who was untrue to Him. His name was Judas.

Now Judas knew that certain people, who did not love Jesus, had been trying to catch Him in some wrong. Yet with all their trying, they could find nothing against Him. They had made up their minds, to take Him to the ruler anyway and ask to have Him put to death. Judas, the untrue disciple, went to some of these enemies of Jesus and made a bargain with them.

He promised that for thirty pieces of silver, he would show them where to find Jesus. And from that time on, he planned how to betray his Master.

One evening when Jesus and His disciples, were all together at supper—the last supper, it is called—Judas slipped away from the table.

Jesus talked earnestly to the others.

He told them that very soon, He was going away, to be with the Father in heaven. It was hard for the disciples to believe, that this would happen to their loving Friend. He helped them to understand, that it was God's will.

"Let not your heart be troubled," said Jesus to them, "In My Father's house are many mansions; I go to prepare a place for you, and if I go and prepare a place for you, I will come again and receive you unto Myself; that where I am, there ye may be also."

He gave them many other loving messages, and they were together for a long time.

Then Jesus prayed to the Father in heaven. Some day you may want to read this prayer and you will find it, in the seventeenth chapter of John.

After the supper was over, Jesus and His disciples sang a hymn and walked out to a garden, where they had often been before.

There Jesus left the disciples and went away by Himself to pray.

Judas knew that Jesus was going out to that garden, so he had told the officers where they would find Him.

To make sure there would be no mistake, Judas had said, "Whomsoever I shall kiss, that is he; take him."

When the soldiers and the mob came into the garden, Judas spoke to Jesus and said, "Hail, Master;" then he kissed Jesus on the cheek.

The loving Saviour looked into the faces of that angry mob and asked, "Whom seek ye?"

"Jesus," they answered.

"I am he," said Jesus.

They drew back in surprise and again Jesus asked them, "Whom seek ye?"

"Jesus of Nazareth," they answered.

"I told you that I am he; if therefore ye seek me, let these go their way."

Then the soldiers seized Jesus roughly and bound Him. They mocked Him and beat Him. They did everything that an angry crowd could do.

THEY TOOK HIM BEFORE THE ROMAN GOVERNOR, PILATE

CHRIST BEFORE PILATE

AS Jesus was hurried from one place to another before the officers, the men were very brutal to Him; they slapped Him and mocked Him.

They wanted Him to be put to death.

Before this could happen, however, they had to take Him before the Roman governor, Pilate.

"What has this man done?" he asked of the mob that howled for Jesus' life, "I find no fault in Him."

Then Jesus' wicked accusers tried to make out that He had sinned in many ways. They said that He had sinned against the Roman emperor, by saying that He was a king.

But Jesus did not mean that He was an earthly king. He had said, "My kingdom is not of this world."

When Pilate heard that Jesus had said He was king of the Jews, he turned to Jesus and said, "Art thou the king of the Jews?" And

Jesus answered, "Thou sayest." The chief priests and elders again accused Him of doing wrong things, but He did not answer.

"Don't you hear what these people are saying against you?" asked Pilate. But even then Jesus did not answer.

There was a great feast going on at the time, and the Roman governor, Pilate, was allowed to free one prisoner during the time of that feast. He saw that Jesus had done nothing that was worthy of death, and he wanted very much to have Jesus released, so he asked, "Whom shall I release to you, Jesus or Barabbas?"

Now Barabbas was a very wicked man who had really been sentenced because of his great crimes. When Pilate said, "Whom shall I release, Jesus or Barabbas" the people shouted, "Release Barabbas! Release Barabbas!"

Pilate still hoped that they might change their minds, and he asked, "What then shall I do with Jesus?"

The jealous priests urged the angry mob to ask that Jesus be crucified, so again they shouted, "Let Him be crucified! Let Him be crucified!"

Pilate did not know what to do. He cried out, "Why should we crucify Him? What evil hath He done? I find no fault in Him."

The crowd answered, "If you let this man go, you are not Caesar's friend."

Pilate knew by that answer, that these people would report him to Caesar, and that he might lose his office of governor.

Poor coward that Pilate was! He took a pan of water and washing his hands, he said to those gathered around him, "I am innocent of the blood of this just person: see ye to it."

He then released the guilty prisoner, Barabbas, and after giving Jesus a hard beating, delivered Him to the mob so that they might crucify Him.

THE CRUCIFIXION

THEN the soldiers of the governor took Jesus into the common hall, and the mob went with them. And they took Him out to the mountainside, where He was to be crucified.

They made Him carry His own cross. It was so heavy that He fell under the weight of it. A man by the name of Simon stepped up to help Him. Finally they reached the place called Golgotha.

In the great crowd that followed, there were many of Jesus' friends, but there were not enough of them to take Him away from His cruel enemies.

His beloved disciples, Peter and Andrew, James and John, Philip and Bartholomew, and all the rest of them were there, but they were helpless. All they could do was to hope and pray, that there might be some way in which they could aid Him.

And they crucified Him, and cast lots for his garments. A crown of thorns was placed upon His brow, the cross was raised in position, and above Jesus' head was placed the inscription, "This is Jesus, King of the Jews."

Then there were two thieves crucified with Him, One on the right hand, and another on the left.

While He was on the cross, the people mocked Him and said ugly things to Him.

Just at noon-time that day, darkness fell over all the earth. The people did not know what to think of this and were afraid. This darkness remained for three long hours.

At the end of the three hours, Jesus cried to the Father in heaven, "My God, My God, why hast thou forsaken me?"

Someone in the crowd dipped a sponge in vinegar and stuck it on a reed and placed it to Jesus' lips. Again He cried to the Father in heaven and the beautiful spirit left His body and He was dead.

AT NOON-TIME THAT DAY, DARKNESS FELL OVER ALL THE EARTH

JESUS LIVING AGAIN

SOON after Jesus died Joseph went to Pilate and begged that he might take Jesus' body to his own tomb.

"I should like to bury Him in a new tomb, which I have just had cut in the rock," said he.

Pilate gave Joseph permission to take the body of Jesus, and Joseph went back to tell the people what Pilate had said.

He and some of the other men took the cross down; they wrapped Jesus' body in linen and they tenderly placed it in the tomb.

One man whose name was Nicodemus, came bringing some of the very finest of spices and perfumes with which to anoint Jesus' body. A great stone was rolled up at the door.

Jesus' mother, Mary, and some of the other women, went to the tomb when He was buried.

It was the very saddest day the earth had ever known.

When the body of Jesus was placed in the tomb, the rulers said among themselves, "We will put soldiers there to guard the door, because Jesus had once said that He would be raised from the dead."

They said: "We will guard His tomb." And so they placed soldiers on each side of the door.

Loving friends of Jesus—Mary, His mother, and Mary Magdalene, and Salome—planned that they would visit the tomb, very early on the first day of the week.

They wanted to take sweet spices, to anoint the body of their loving Friend and Master.

It was not yet daylight when they started out to go to the tomb. As they walked along they spoke very softly about Jesus; they talked about His goodness and they wondered how His enemies, could ever have taken Him and treated Him the way they did.

As they went closer to the tomb they said to each other: "Who will roll away the stone from the door?" But when they reached the door of the tomb, they found that the stone had been rolled away!

An angel from heaven sat upon the stone. His clothes were as white as snow and a beautiful white light shone about him.

The soldiers who guarded the tomb were just like dead men and they could not move or speak.

The angel looked at the women and said these words: "Fear not for I know that ye seek Jesus. He is not here; for He is risen, even as He said. Come see the place where the Lord lay."

The angel then told the women to go quickly and tell His disciples, that Jesus was risen from the dead and that they should go into Galilee to see Him.

The women were so glad and happy, that they quickly ran to tell the disciples.

"And as they went to tell His disciples, behold Jesus met them, saying, All Hail. Then said Jesus unto them, Be not afraid: go tell my brethren that they go into Galilee, and there they shall see me."

THE WALK TO EMMAUS

ON the very afternoon of the Sunday, when the women had gone to the tomb of Jesus and found His body no longer there, two of His dear friends set out to walk to Emmaus a village about seven miles from Jerusalem.

One of them was called Cleopas, but the Bible does not tell us the name of the other.

There had been a great deal of excitement in Jerusalem that day, when the news spread that Jesus had risen from the dead. Some believed the story and some did not.

These two friends of Jesus, were talking over everything that had happened since Friday, that sad day when Jesus had been nailed to the cross.

They were greatly troubled and did not know what to think, or to do next.

As they walked along, absorbed in their talk, some one joined them.

It was Jesus, but they did not recognize Him. He was not yet ready to let them know who He was.

"What are you talking about so earnestly?" He asked.

"You must be a stranger," answered Cleopas. "Don't you know what has happened in Jerusalem?"

"What?" asked Jesus.

Then they told Him all about the great, good Man, who had been so cruelly treated.

"We had hoped that He would redeem Israel," they said:

"It is now the third day since these things came to pass.

"Some of the women of our company amazed us by going early to the tomb.

"They did not find His body there and they saw angels who said, 'He is alive.'

"Some of the disciples also went up to the tomb and found everything just as the women had said, but they did not see Jesus."

"Ought not Christ to have suffered these things and to enter into His glory?" Jesus said to them. Then as they walked along, He explained many things, that had been written about Himself in the Scriptures.

Jesus had not yet made Himself known to the two friends, when they reached the end of their journey.

As He seemed about to leave them to go on further, they begged Him to stay saying, "Abide with us, for it is toward evening and the day is now far spent."

Jesus gladly went into the house and soon after, they sat down to supper together.

When Jesus took the bread and blessed it, the eyes of the men were opened and they knew Him and He vanished out of their sight.

The men said to each other, "Why didn't we know it was Jesus; nobody else could have explained things as He did."

They were so excited and happy, that they started back to Jerusalem, with their joyful news.

They found the eleven disciples together and as happy as they.

"Jesus is risen indeed and hath appeared to Simon Peter," the disciples cried out. Then Cleopas and his friend, told the wonderful thing that had happened to them, on their way to Emmaus.

DOUBTING THOMAS

AFTER Jesus had risen from the dead, He appeared to some of the disciples but Thomas was not with them. A short time after, when Thomas came in, the others said to him, "Thomas, we have seen the Lord."

Thomas could not believe it; "Except I shall see in His hands the print of the nails," he said, "and put my finger into the print of the nails, and put my hand into His side, I will not believe."

About eight days later, the disciples were again in the same room and Thomas was with them. While the doors were shut, Jesus stood among them and greeted them with these words, "Peace be unto you."

He looked at Thomas and said, "Thomas, reach hither thy finger, and see my hands; reach hither thy hand, and put it into my side, and be not faithless, but believing."

Thomas looked at Jesus. "My Lord and my God," he cried out.

Then Jesus said to Thomas, "Because thou hast seen me, thou hast believed: blessed are they that have not seen, and yet have believed."

Thomas never doubted Jesus again.

THEN PETER REACHED OUT HIS HAND TO THE BEGGAR AND HELPED HIM UP

A BEGGAR AT THE BEAUTIFUL GATE

ONCE there was a man, who had been lame all his life.
When he was only a tiny child, his mother had tried to teach him to walk. She found that his little feet were crooked and that his ankle bones were not strong enough to hold the weight of his body.

No doctor could help the poor child and his little legs never grew any stronger.

He could not run and play like other boys; he had to sit by quietly and watch the others.

When he grew older, there was only one way he could get his living: that was by begging.

Every day his friends carried him to the temple and laid him by a gate called, "The Beautiful Gate."

Many people passed through this gate on their way to the temple. Some of them slipped coins into the lame man's hands as they went by.

One day as he was sitting in his usual place, two men, a very young man and one much older, drew near the gate on their way to the temple.

They were Peter and John, two of Jesus' most beloved disciples. Jesus had gone to His home in heaven and these men were trying their best, to carry on His work on earth. They were happy, that Jesus had loved them well enough, to trust His work to them.

They were thinking of Jesus this day, when they drew near The Beautiful Gate and saw the lame man holding out his hands for alms.

Peter, the older of the two men, looked straight into the man's face and said to him, "Look on us."

The lame man obeyed thinking that they were going to give him something.

"Silver and gold have I none," said Peter, "but what I have—that I give thee. In the name of Jesus Christ of Nazareth, rise up and walk."

Then Peter reached out his hand to the beggar and helped him up. At once the man found he could stand on his feet and he began to walk and leap!

His first thought was to go into the temple and praise God. As he went walking and leaping, the people gathered there looked at him and said, "Isn't this the same man that sat at the gate and begged for alms?"

The poor man was so happy, he hardly knew what to do; he clung closely to Peter and John and would not let them go.

The people, astonished by the wonderful change in the man, crowded around the two disciples.

Peter told them that they must not think that he and John had cured the lame man. "It is God's power," he said, "that has made this man well."

PHILIP AND THE ETHIOPIAN

AMONG the faithful helpers, who were trying to carry on the work of Jesus in Jerusalem, was one by the name of Philip.

Philip was much startled one day when an angel came to him with a message from heaven.

"Go toward the South, Philip," said the angel, "unto the way that goeth down from Jerusalem to Gaza."

Philip knew that this command came from God and he obeyed it at once. As he traveled toward the South, he saw a fine chariot rolling along the road. In the chariot sat a dark-skinned man, reading from a scroll.

The stranger in the chariot came from a country called Ethiopia. He was a man of importance there, as he had charge of the treasure of its queen, Candace. He had been to Jerusalem to worship and was on his way home.

As Philip saw the Ethiopian, God's spirit said to him, "Go near and join thyself to this chariot."

Philip ran toward the chariot at once and heard the man reading these words:

"He was led as a sheep to the slaughter, and as a lamb before his shearers is dumb, so he opened not his mouth."

Philip knew that they were written about Jesus, by the Prophet Isaiah.

"Do you understand what you are reading?" he asked the stranger.

The man answered, "No I do not understand, for there is no one to explain it to me. Won't you come up and sit beside me and tell me what it means?"

Philip climbed into the chariot and as they rode along, Philip told the Ethiopian about Jesus and His love for all the world.

He explained that the line, "as a lamb before his shearers is dumb, so he opened not his mouth," meant that Jesus, when taken before the great Judge Pilate, made no complaint against his persecutors.

The Ethiopian listened while Philip told him how Jesus had suffered, how He had died on the cross, and had gone home to heaven.

He told him, too, of Jesus' command to all His helpers, to go into all the world and make new disciples. Baptizing them in the name of the Father, and of the Son, and of the Holy Spirit.

As they drove along, they came to a pool of water.

"See," said the Ethiopian, "here is water, what doth hinder me to be baptized?"

"If thou believest with all thine heart, thou mayest," answered Philip.

"I believe that Jesus Christ is the Son of God," the Ethiopian replied.

They stopped the chariot and Philip took the man down to the pool and baptized him.

When they came back from the water, Philip suddenly disappeared. The Ethiopian climbed into his chariot and went home rejoicing in his new faith.

DORCAS CARRIED JOY WHEREVER SHE WENT

DORCAS, A FRIEND OF THE POOR

JUST a few miles from the city of Jerusalem, there is a seaport called Joppa.

There were many poor people in that city. Often they did not have enough to eat or wear.

There were many widows too, whose little children were ragged and hungry.

In Joppa there lived a good, kind-hearted woman, whose name was Dorcas.

The Bible says she was "full of good works and alms deeds." She visited strangers in the city to see if they needed help.

Dorcas was very clever with her needle. If she noticed that a little boy or girl needed a coat or a dress, she would cut and sew, until she had a neat little garment for the child. Often she carried tasty food to a family when the mother was too ill to prepare any.

Dorcas carried joy wherever she went and everyone loved her dearly.

One day all Joppa was sad. Good, kind Dorcas was very ill. The little children, asked for her in anxious voices. Then came the news that she was dead.

The people were grieving very deeply, when some one happened to think of Peter, one of Jesus' good helpers, who was in a nearby town, Lydda.

"Peter cured a sick man in Lydda," said one man. And some one else added, "And Peter cured a lame man at the Beautiful Gate. He had been lame all his life, too. Maybe Peter could help us. Let us ask him to come to Joppa to see Dorcas."

So two men were sent to Lydda to get Peter. He came back with them gladly and went directly to the home of Dorcas.

In the upper room where she lay, there were gathered many poor widows weeping.

They crowded around Peter, showing him the garments Dorcas, had made for themselves and their children.

Peter asked them all to go out of the room; then he knelt down and prayed; he spoke to Dorcas saying, "Dorcas, arise."

Dorcas opened her eyes and looked around; when she saw Peter, she sat up.

"Peter gave her his hand and lifted her up, and when he had called the saints and widows, presented her alive."

How happy they were to see their good, kind friend again!

It did not take very long, for the word to go all over the city. When the people thanked Peter, he told them that it was God's power not his, that had raised Dorcas from the dead.

STEPHEN

AFTER the death of Jesus, His disciples stayed in Jerusalem for a long time and tried to carry out His wishes.

So many came to believe in Him, that new helpers were needed. Seven fine young men were chosen. Stephen was one of them. He was an able, earnest and charming young man. The Bible says of him: "Stephen, full of faith and power, did great wonders and miracles among the people."

But Stephen did not preach very long. The enemies of Jesus' followers, began to make trouble for this earnest young worker. They even bribed men, to tell untrue stories about him.

One day some of his enemies seized Stephen and took him before the council. They accused him of saying wicked things about God and about the laws of Moses. As they looked at Stephen, they saw that his face shone, like the face of an angel.

Stephen began to speak. He told them the whole story of God's love for them and of His sending Jesus. And he told them that they had killed God's son.

When they heard these words, they were very angry. But Stephen's face was still shining, for he was filled with God's spirit. He looked up into heaven and said:

"Behold, I see the heavens opened, and the Son of man standing on the right hand of God."

Then, as the Bible says, "the people and the council cried out with a loud voice, and stopped their ears and ran upon him with one accord and cast him out of the city, and stoned him: and the witnesses laid down their clothes at a young man's feet whose name was Saul."

While these wicked people stoned Stephen he prayed, "Lord Jesus, receive my spirit."

As the cruel stones came faster and faster, he knelt down, and cried in a loud voice, "Lord, lay not this sin to their charge."

Then he died.

ANANIAS AND SAPPHIRA

AFTER the glad, great day in Jerusalem, when so many came to believe in Jesus, His church grew and grew.

Some of these believers were rich and some were very poor. They felt that they were like one big family and that whatever anyone owned should be shared.

Those who had houses and lands, sold them and brought the money to Jesus' helpers and they gave it out as it was needed. They thought this was the best way, of showing their love for Jesus.

One man, Barnabas, who had a big field worth a great deal of money, sold the field and took every bit of his money to the helpers of Jesus.

But all were not as honorable as Barnabas.

Ananias made a plan with his wife, Sapphira, that they would just pretend to do as the others did. They would sell their land and keep back part of the money, and give Jesus' helpers only a part of it.

So they sold their land and put some of the money away. Then Ananias went to the disciples and carried the rest of the money. He laid it down at their feet, and pretended it was all he had.

But Peter knew better, and he said, "Ananias, why has Satan filled your heart to lie to the Holy Ghost, and to keep back part of the price of the land?

"It was your own land and you might have kept it. After it was sold it was in your own power. You were not asked to do this. You have not lied unto men, but unto God."

Then Ananias fell down dead. The young men that were there, wound his garments around him and carried him out and buried him.

Three hours after this, Sapphira, the wife of Ananias, went to the disciples, not knowing what had happened to her husband.

"Did you sell the land for so much?" said Peter to her, and she answered, "Yes, for so much."

Then Peter said to her, "You and Ananias have agreed together to tempt the spirit of the Lord. Behold the feet of them which buried thy husband are at the door and shall carry thee out."

Sapphira dropped dead too and was buried beside her husband.

PAUL AND SILAS IN PRISON

AFTER Stephen was killed, some of the believers went to the city of Antioch. Paul and Barnabas were two of their earnest preachers.

God sent a message to these Christians at Antioch, telling them to send Paul and Barnabas out as missionaries.

They were sent and worked together for a long, long time.

Later Paul decided that he would take Silas with him, and that Barnabas and John Mark should go together.

While Paul and Silas were working together, a very strange thing happened. One night as Paul lay asleep, a man stood by his couch.

"Come over into Macedonia," said the man, "and help us."

Paul knew that God had sent this message to him, and he and Silas made ready to go at once.

Soon they came to a city called Philippi and stayed there for several days.

One day they met a slave girl, who seemed to have the power of telling fortunes. In this way, she made a great deal of money for her masters.

This girl kept following Paul and Silas and calling after them. At length Paul could stand it no longer and he commanded the bad spirit in her to come out. After that, she could no longer tell fortunes.

Her masters were very angry. They seized the two missionaries and dragged them into the public square before the city officials. There they accused them of being trouble makers.

The angry officials tore the clothes from Paul and Silas. They had them cruelly beaten, until there were stripes and welts upon their bodies. At last they threw them into prison.

The jailor thrust their feet in stocks and locked them in the inner prison.

The two missionaries, forgetting their bruised and bleeding bodies, were praying and singing hymns to God. Suddenly a great earthquake shook the prison to its very foundations.

All the doors of the prison were opened, and the chains fell from the prisoners.

The jailor, wakened out of his sleep, saw the doors wide open. He knew that if the prisoners were gone he would be punished, and he drew his sword to take his own life. But Paul called to him, "Do thyself no harm, for we are all here."

Then the jailor, trembling and frightened, fell down before Paul and Silas and cried out, "Sirs, what must I do to be saved?"

"You must believe in Jesus Christ," they said, and then they told him all about Jesus. He and all his household believed and were baptized.

The jailor was very kind to Paul and Silas. He bathed their bruised bodies, and took them to his home and gave them food.

The very next day, the city officials set Paul and Silas free. They went then to the home of a Christian woman whose name was Lydia, and talked of Jesus to many who were gathered there.

Then they went away from Philippi into another city.

PAUL WENT TO PHILIPPI AS A MISSIONARY

PAUL IN EPHESUS

PAUL, the great missionary, came at one time to a city called Ephesus. There he found many followers of Jesus. There were many others, however, who worshipped a great goddess called Diana. They made images of her and prayed to them. They had built for her, one of the most beautiful temples in the world, the Temple of Diana.

Paul told them that it was wrong to pray to idols. Many listened to him and many more did not.

There were silversmiths at Ephesus, who earned their living by making models of the Temple of Diana.

One of them, named Demetrius, called all the others together and said to them, "Do you see how this man, Paul, is preaching and turning the people away from Diana by telling them, 'There is no god made with hands?'

"Not only will our business be ruined but Diana will no longer be worshipped as a great goddess."

When the silversmiths heard this they cried out, "Great is Diana of the Ephesians!"

The others took up the cry—and there was a great riot. The people all rushed into the theatre, dragging two of Paul's traveling companions with them. Paul wanted to follow, but the disciples were not willing that he should.

Inside there was great excitement. Some shouted one thing and some another and most of them did not know why they had come.

For two hours they kept shouting, "Great is Diana of the Ephesians! Great is Diana of the Ephesians!"

At last an officer quieted them saying, "There is no cause for this uproar. Everybody knows you worship Diana.

"Ye have brought hither these men, which are neither robbers of churches nor yet blasphemers of your goddess.

"Now if Demetrius wants to bring charges against them, the law is open, and let him do it in a lawful way.

"We are in danger to be called in question for this day's uproar," and with these words he sent them away.

After the uproar was over, Paul said goodbye to his helpers and went out of their city.

PAUL'S SHIPWRECK

WHEN Paul was in deep trouble he went before the king, whose name was Agrippa, and told him about it. King Agrippa, after hearing Paul's story, said that Paul had done nothing to deserve imprisonment or death. But Paul's enemies did not want to let him go free and they insisted that he be tried.

Paul asked that his trial be held in Rome, and at last it was decided to send him there.

This meant a long journey, for Rome was a city far away, across the great Mediterranean Sea.

The ship on which Paul was sent, was caught in a terrible storm. For days neither sun nor stars could be seen. The wind blew furiously and the ship was so battered by the waves, that the sailors began to lighten it, by throwing out some of the cargo and even the ropes. At last they gave up all hope, of ever seeing land again. Then Paul stood up among the frightened men and spoke these comforting words:

"Be of good cheer, for no one among you shall lose his life; nothing will be lost but the ship."

Then Paul told them, that in the night, one of God's angels had stood by him and said, "Fear not, Paul, thou must be brought before Caesar; and, lo, God hath given thee all them that sail with thee."

He urged them to forget their fears, for he knew that God would do as He had said.

After fourteen days of drifting about, the sailors thought they were nearing land; they measured the depth of the water and found that it was very shallow. They were afraid they would be wrecked on the rocks, so they threw out four anchors and waited for daylight.

Just before dawn Paul spoke to them all again and begged them to take some food, for they had not eaten for many days. And he comforted them once more saying: "For there shall not a hair fall from the head of any of you."

Then he took bread and gave thanks to God for it; he broke it and began to eat.

Greatly cheered they all began to eat too.

When it was day, no one could make out what land they had reached. It was decided to run the ship ashore, in a little creek. The sailors cut away the anchors and untied the rudder. Then they hoisted the sail and made for the beach. But alas, the ship ran aground. The bow stuck fast and could not be moved, but the stern began to break up, as the waves beat upon it.

There were two hundred and seventy-six people on board and many of them were prisoners, who were being taken to Rome.

The soldiers wanted to kill the prisoners, for fear they would swim ashore and escape. But the officer put a stop to this plan, because he wished to save Paul, who had done so much for them.

He ordered all those who could swim, to jump overboard and swim to land. The rest followed clinging to boards and broken pieces of the ship.

In this way they all got safely to land. But the ship was broken to pieces.

The island on which they were cast was called Melita (Malta). The islanders treated the shipwrecked men with great kindness.

THE SHIP WAS BROKEN TO PIECES

Paul hearing that the father of the ruler was very sick, went to see him and prayed to God, to bring him back to health. And God answered Paul's prayer.

Many other sick people came to Paul and were cured of their illnesses.

After spending three months on the island of Melita, the shipwrecked men set out again for Rome.

A SLAVE WHO RAN AWAY

ONESIMUS was a young slave, who lived many hundreds of years ago, in a far away country. His master Philemon was a good man, yet Onesimus longed to be free.

He thought if he could only get to the big city of Rome, no one there would know that he was a slave.

So he ran away, taking some of his master's money, for his expenses.

Onesimus finally reached Rome safely. While he was living there, he went to hear a great preacher. This preacher was the famous missionary Paul, who had been taken to Rome as a prisoner.

Though a prisoner, Paul was allowed to go on with his preaching. He taught people how to make their lives better. He told them the wonderful story of Jesus; how He had come to earth and lived among the people. And he told them how Jesus had suffered and died on the cross and had gone home to heaven.

When the slave, Onesimus, heard this story he felt ashamed of the way in which he had behaved: he knew now that he had done wrong in running away from his master.

He did not know quite what he ought to do, so he decided to go to the good man Paul and tell him his story.

Paul saw that Onesimus was not just a common slave. He felt that he would make a fine man and a good leader. He had run away because he had known no better.

"You ought to go back to Philemon, Onesimus," said Paul to him one day, "and tell him that you made a mistake and are sorry."

"I don't believe Philemon will be hard on you," said Paul, "for he is one of God's followers—a good Christian."

"I will write a letter to him and ask him to let you come back to Rome with me, for you will be very useful here in my work."

Onesimus was glad to do as Paul advised. Paul wrote a beautiful letter to Philemon, asking him to let Onesimus come back to Rome, to be with him.

In the letter he told Philemon that he loved him very much and prayed for him always, and he added, "I have much joy and comfort in thy love."

Then he wrote Philemon that he was sending back Onesimus, although he had become very dear to him and would be most helpful in his work. He said that he wanted to keep him, but that he would not do so without Philemon's consent. And he went on to say:

"If he hath wronged thee or oweth to thee aught put that on mine account, I, Paul, have written it with mine own hand; I will repay it."

When the letter was finished, Paul sent Onesimus home to Philemon. Philemon was glad to let the runaway slave go back to Rome again, to be Paul's faithful helper.

JOHN'S VISION ON THE ISLAND OF PATMOS

ONE day while Jesus was walking by the Lake of Galilee, He stopped to talk with some fishermen. Before He left them He said, "Leave your nets and follow me."

The young men on the shore were Peter and Andrew, James and John.

You have had many stories about the things which all of these helpers of Jesus did, and you know how faithful they were to Jesus' work.

John, however, was always by His side, and so he was called the "beloved disciple." Many times you have seen him pictured with Jesus.

On the night when Jesus was having His last supper with His friends in the upper room, John sat at the table and leaned his head against Jesus' breast.

When Jesus was hanging on the cross John stood at the foot of it and near him stood Jesus' own mother, Mary.

Jesus spoke to John and said, "Behold thy Mother," that was His way of telling John to take care of Mary always.

A BEAUTIFUL PICTURE CAME BEFORE HIM—IT WAS A PICTURE OF HEAVEN

After Jesus' death John was true and strong; he endured many hardships. He and Peter were put in prison; they were beaten and cruelly treated. They did not mind it because they were doing it all for Jesus' sake.

Just before Jesus died He had said to Peter and John and the others, "I go to prepare a place for you: in my Father's house are many mansions."

Nobody knows, of course, but we just like to think that the Father and the Son together planned the beautiful mansions of heaven.

One time John did something again that did not please the rulers of the country, and they said, "Because you have gone on teaching in a way that we told you not to do, we are going to send you away to the island of Patmos. You can never come back to this country again."

So John was banished to the island of Patmos.

One day as he was looking over the sea and talking to God, a very beautiful picture came before him—it was a picture of heaven.

Then a Great Voice spoke to him and told him many things that could be seen and many things that would be given to those who tried to do God's will.

As John looked there appeared a great light, more beautiful than he had ever seen, more beautiful than the light of the sun or the moon or the stars.

The picture of heaven with all its lovely mansions came before John. He said there was a great wall all around the city and that it was set with precious stones of all kinds. In the walls were twelve gates and these gates were all of pearl.

They were the most beautiful things anyone could think of.

There was one angel at every gate to guard the going in.

The city itself was of pure gold.

If you were to think of the most beautiful thing you have ever seen, you could not think of anything so wonderful.

John said that there was no need of the sun or the moon or the stars, for there was no night.

He said that through the streets of the city, there flowed the most beautiful river that could be thought of, whose water was just as clear as crystal.

Everything in the city was pure and clean, there was nothing that was unclean or ugly.

Different kinds of fruit trees that gave fruit every month in the year were along the river bank.

As John looked at the picture he wrote of the things that he saw, so that men and women, boys and girls might read about them.

Some day you will want to read all of this in the book of Revelation, the very last book in the Bible. Then you will remember what a lovable man John was, and you will want to be like him because he was always working for Jesus.

May the Lord bless you & keep you
May the Lord make his face to shine upon you and be gracious unto you
May the Lord lift his countenance upon you & give you peace.   Amen

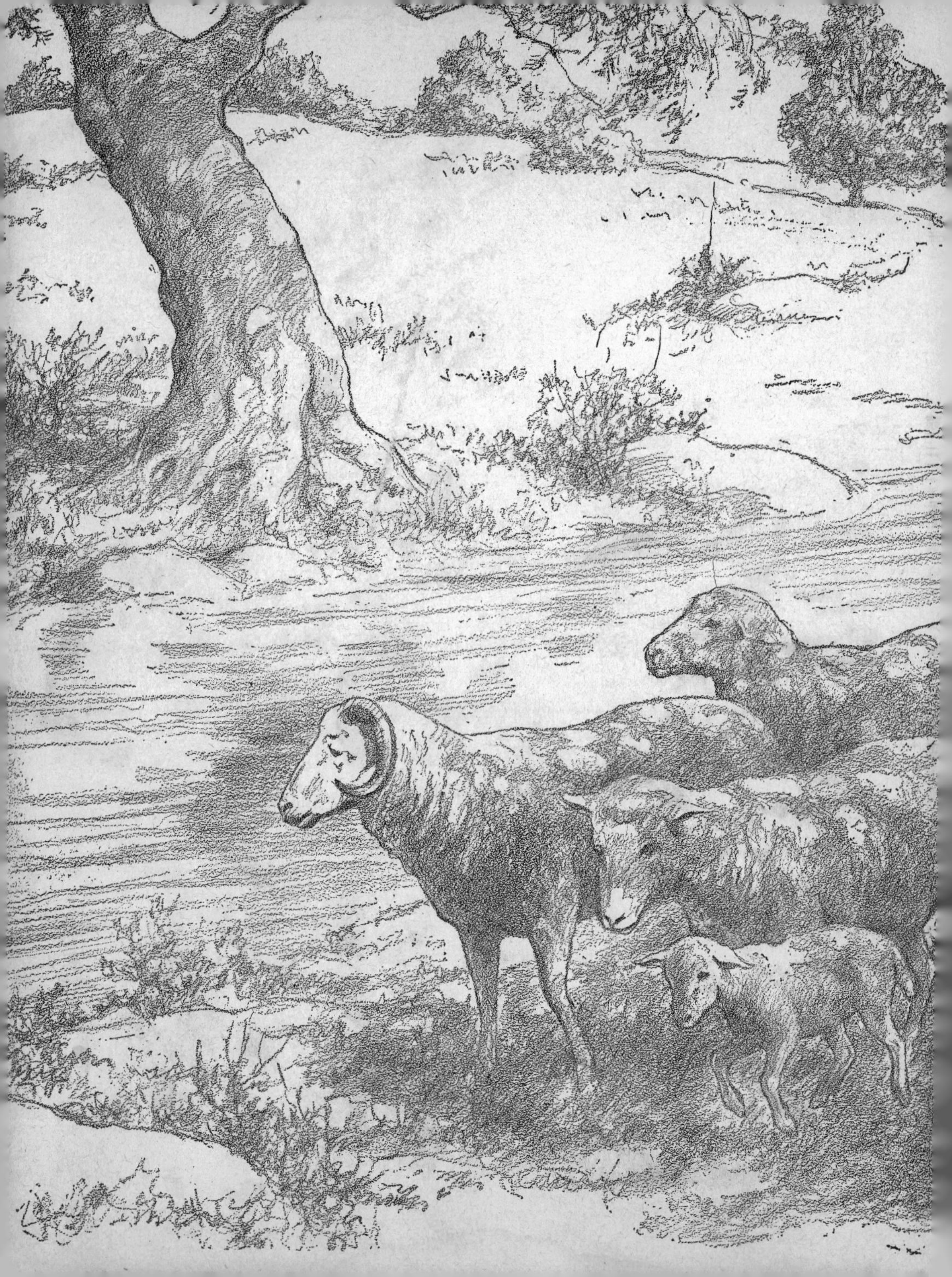